Iran

BLAINE WISEMAN

MEDIA ENHANCED BOOKS
AV2 BY WEIGL
ADDED VALUE • AUDIO VISUAL

www.av2books.com

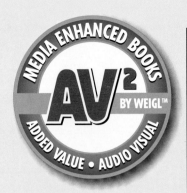

Go to **www.av2books.com**, and enter this book's unique code.

BOOK CODE

M 5 4 7 9 1 5

AV² by Weigl brings you media enhanced books that support active learning.

AV² provides enriched content that supplements and complements this book. Weigl's AV² books strive to create inspired learning and engage young minds in a total learning experience.

Your AV² Media Enhanced books come alive with...

Audio
Listen to sections of the book read aloud.

Key Words
Study vocabulary, and complete a matching word activity.

Video
Watch informative video clips.

Quizzes
Test your knowledge.

Embedded Weblinks
Gain additional information for research.

Slide Show
View images and captions, and prepare a presentation.

Try This!
Complete activities and hands-on experiments.

... and much, much more!

Published by AV² by Weigl
350 5th Avenue, 59th Floor
New York, NY 10118
Website: www.av2books.com

Library of Congress Cataloging-in-Publication Data

Names: Wiseman, Blaine, author.
Title: Iran / Blaine Wiseman.
Other titles: Exploring countries (AV2 by Weigl)
Description: New York, NY : AV2 by Weigl, 2017. | Series: Exploring countries
  | Includes bibliographical references and index.
Identifiers: LCCN 2016047219 (print) | LCCN 2016052649 (ebook) | ISBN
  9781489654113 (hard cover : alk. paper) | ISBN 9781489654120 (soft cover :
  alk. paper) | ISBN 9781489654137 (Multi-user ebk.)
Subjects: LCSH: Iran--History--Juvenile literature. |
  Iran--Civilization--Juvenile literature.
Classification: LCC DS254.75 .W57 2017 (print) | LCC DS254.75 (ebook) | DDC
  955--dc23
LC record available at https://lccn.loc.gov/2016047219

Printed in the United States of America in Brainerd, Minnesota
1 2 3 4 5 6 7 8 9   21 20 19 18 17

022017
020117

Project Coordinator Heather Kissock
Art Director Terry Paulhus

Photo Credits
Every reasonable effort has been made to trace ownership and to obtain permission to reprint copyright material. The publishers would be pleased to have any errors or omissions brought to their attention so that they may be corrected in subsequent printings.

Weigl acknowledges Getty Images as its primary photo supplier for this title.

Contents

Iran Overview

The country of Iran is located in the Middle East. For thousands of years, Iran was called Persia. It was the home of several ancient **empires**. Historic trade routes between Asia and Europe passed through the region. As a result, Iran's population includes people from many cultural groups. Present-day Iran is an **Islamic** state. Large deposits of natural gas and petroleum, or oil, help to make the nation an economic and political leader in the Middle East.

Dromedary camels, which have one hump, have been used in Iran for almost 2,000 years to carry people and goods. They can tolerate the high temperatures and lack of water in Iranian deserts.

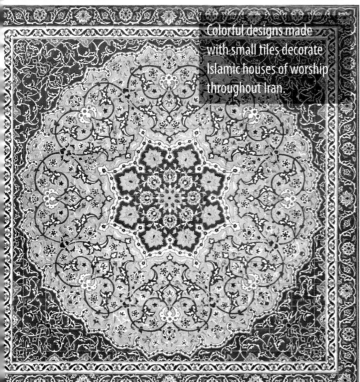

Colorful designs made with small tiles decorate Islamic houses of worship throughout Iran.

Women of the Bandari cultural group in southern Iran cover their faces with masks called burqas.

Many girls in Iran wear traditional garments called chadors, even while playing sports.

Iranians eat a kind of large flatbread called taftoon.

Exploring Iran

With a total area of 636,372 square miles (1,648,195 square kilometers), Iran is the second-largest country in the Middle East, after Saudi Arabia. To the west, Iran borders Iraq and Turkey. To the north, it borders Armenia, Azerbaijan, the Caspian Sea, and Turkmenistan. In the east, Iran shares borders with Afghanistan and Pakistan. Iran's southern border stretches 1,100 miles (1,770 km) along the Persian Gulf and the Gulf of Oman. Just across the water are several oil-rich countries in the Arabian Peninsula, including Saudi Arabia, Kuwait, the United Arab Emirates, and Oman.

Black Sea

Turkey

Tehran

Syria

Jordan

Kavir Desert

Red Sea

N

Map Legend

Iran

Land

Water

▲ Mount Damāvand

Kavir Desert

Persian Gulf

📍 Capital City

SCALE

250 Miles

250 Kilometers

Tehran

Tehran is the capital and largest city in Iran. More than 8 million people live there. The city is a business and financial center.

Uzbekistan

Azerbaijan

Armenia

Turkmenistan

Mount Damāvand

Tehran

Kavir Desert

Afghanistan

IRAN

Iraq

Kuwait

Pakistan

Strait of Hormuz

Persian Gulf

Gulf of Oman

United Arab Emirates

Persian Gulf

Oman

Saudi Arabia

Kavir Desert

The Kavir Desert is Iran's largest desert. It is located in the northern part of the country. The desert's surface has a salt crust, caused by the lack of rain and by the evaporation of water from salt marshes.

Persian Gulf

The Persian Gulf is a long, narrow waterway with an area of about 93,000 square miles (241,000 sq. km). It is a major shipping route for oil and other products. The Strait of Hormuz at its southern end connects the gulf to the Gulf of Oman and the Indian Ocean.

Mount Damāvand

At 18,406 feet (5,620 meters), Mount Damāvand is Iran's tallest mountain. It is part of the Elburz Mountains. An active volcano, it last erupted more than 7,000 years ago.

LAND AND CLIMATE

Towering mountains, barren deserts, and coastal lowlands can all be found in Iran. In the center of the country is a high **plateau**. Iran's largest deserts, the Kavir and the Lut, are located on the plateau. Parts of these deserts receive no rain for months at a time. Lake Urmia, a saltwater lake, is located in northwestern Iran. It is the largest lake in the Middle East.

A series of mountain ranges border the central plateau. To the north, the Elburz Mountains extend east–west across northern Iran. To the west, near the Persian Gulf, the Zagros Mountains stretch from Turkey to the Strait of Hormuz. Iran is the site of frequent earthquakes, and some of its mountains are volcanoes. This is due to the country's location, where two of Earth's **tectonic plates** meet.

Salt deposits form on the shores of Lake Urmia, one of the largest saltwater lakes in the world.

North of the Elburz Mountains, the **elevation** of the land drops sharply in a 70-mile (115-km) wide area that borders the Caspian Sea. There is a similar change in elevation near Iran's western coast. In that region, the land drops by 2,000 feet (600 m) as it slopes toward the Persian Gulf and Gulf of Oman.

Iran's varied landscapes result in great differences in precipitation. The country's mountains block clouds from carrying moisture to the central plateau. In the southeastern portion of the plateau, rainfall averages less than 2 inches (5 centimeters) per year. In the area near the Caspian Sea, the yearly average is 78 inches (198 cm). Temperatures vary greatly, too, often depending on elevation. In the city of Tabriz, which is 4,485 feet (1,367 m) above sea level in northwestern Iran, temperatures fall as low as 23° Fahrenheit (−2° Celsius). In the lowlands near the Caspian Sea, temperatures can reach 100°F (38°C) or more.

The Baladeh region in north-central Iran lies on the north side of the Elburz Mountains, near the Caspian Sea.

115°F (46°C)

Temperature recorded at the Iranian city of Bandar Mahshahr, on the Persian Gulf coast, on July 31, 2015, during a heat wave.

One-Third Portion of Iran's border that is seacoast.

13 Number of earthquakes in Iran during the 1900s in which the death toll was 1,500 or higher.

PLANTS AND ANIMALS

Different types of plants and animals have **adapted** to the conditions in each of Iran's landscapes. At higher elevations, there are oak and elm trees, as well as other trees and shrubs that can thrive in colder climates. Animals living in highland regions include the Iranian jerboa, a rodent **species** found only in Iran. Large animals such as the mouflon, a type of big-horned sheep, and the Eurasian brown bear roam Iran's highland slopes and forests.

Many plants in Iran's deserts can thrive in a dry climate. Shrubs and grasses have roots that take in water stored underground to help the plants survive. Desert **oases** support larger plants including poplar trees. The **endangered** Asiatic cheetah lives in Iran's deserts, as well as birds such as buzzards and Iranian ground jays. Lowland areas near the Caspian Sea are home to lush forests. The Caspian Sea and Persian Gulf support a wide variety of sea life, from tiny shrimp to large sturgeon.

Urial, a type of sheep native to Iran, now live mostly in protected areas in the northeastern part of the country.

NATURAL RESOURCES

158 Billion Barrels
Iran's estimated oil reserves.
(25 trillion liters)

1st Iran's rank, according to some estimates, among nations with reserves of natural gas.

10% Portion of Iran's land that is covered by forests.

Iran's oil and natural gas **reserves** are its most valuable natural resources. Saudi Arabia is the only Middle Eastern country with more oil. Iran holds almost 10 percent of the world's oil reserves and more than 15 percent of its gas reserves. Iran uses these fuels to power its industries, homes, and vehicles. The country also sells oil and gas to other nations, which brings money into Iran.

Metals and minerals are mined throughout Iran, especially in highland and mountainous areas. Copper and zinc are two major resources. Iron, coal, uranium, and gold are also mined.

In some parts of the country, rich soil is an important resource. Only one-fifth of Iran's land can be used for growing crops, but this land feeds millions of Iranians. Wheat, rice, pistachio nuts, and fruits are important crops. The region near the Caspian Sea is the country's main crop-growing area. Forests in the Caspian Sea region supply Iranians with lumber for buildings and furniture.

Iranian farmers grow about 2 million tons (1.8 million metric tons) of rice per year. Some farmers use machines that separate the grains of rice from the stalks.

TOURISM

Ancient buildings and cultural attractions bring visitors to Iran from all over the world. Several million people travel to Iran each year. Many of these are **Shiite** Muslims who visit for religious reasons. For decades, Iran has had tense relations with the United States and many European nations, and few Americans or Europeans visited. After relations improved somewhat in 2015, tourism from the United States and Europe began to slowly increase.

Tehran's Azadi Tower stands 164 feet (50 m) high.

One of the most visited tourist destinations in Iran is the city of Esfahan. Its mosques, or Muslim houses of worship, are beautiful examples of Islamic **architecture**. Peaceful gardens and graceful bridges also make Esfahan the most picturesque Iranian city.

Most tourists arriving in Iran by plane fly into Tehran, a center of Iranian culture. The city's Azadi, or Freedom, Tower is considered the gateway to Iran. It is made of white marble. Tourists also enjoy the Grand Bazaar. It has been in operation for about 1,000 years. Visitors wander through its streets, shopping for clothing, jewelry, carpets, and spices.

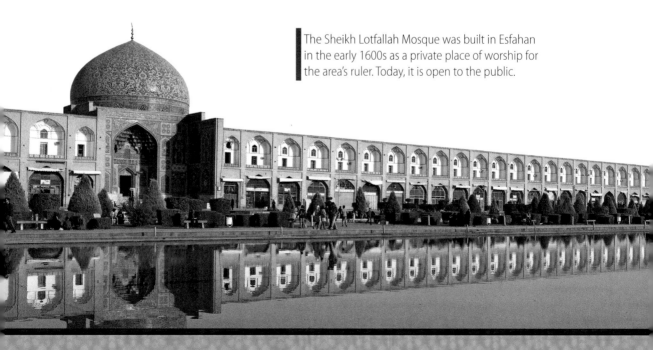

The Sheikh Lotfallah Mosque was built in Esfahan in the early 1600s as a private place of worship for the area's ruler. Today, it is open to the public.

The city of Yazd is a popular attraction for tourists interested in Iran's history and architecture. Located between the Kavir and Lut Deserts, Yazd is the center of Zoroastrianism in Iran. This was the main religion in the country before Islam. Yazd's Zoroastrian fire temple, Ateshkadeh, is home to an eternal flame. It has been burning for more than 1,000 years. The city also features buildings with badgirs, or wind towers. These towers allow cool winds to flow through them. They offer relief from the desert heat.

Persepolis is another well-known tourist destination. Built about 2,500 years ago, it was the capital city of the ancient Achaemenian Empire. Now, Persepolis lies in ruins. Located in a remote mountainous area of southwestern Iran, Persepolis was abandoned for centuries and became covered by soil and sand. Parts of the ancient city have been excavated, or dug out, and restored, giving visitors an indication of Persepolis's past glory.

The Aghazadeh Palace in Yazd is well known for its wind towers.

INDUSTRY

Iran has the second-largest **economy** in the Middle East, after Saudi Arabia. Oil and natural gas production and processing is the country's largest industry. Compared to oil deposits in some other countries, Iran's oil is easy to reach and can be extracted at low cost. This has helped to make the industry profitable. In the early 2000s, economic **sanctions** by the United States and European countries reduced Iran's oil **exports** and hurt the country's economy. Many of these sanctions were eased in 2016.

Iran is the biggest automobile manufacturer in the Middle East. It produced nearly one million cars in 2015. This industry was also harmed by the economic sanctions that were partly lifted in 2016. Since then, the government has been working to expand auto production and exports.

Iran has a long history of producing fabrics and rugs. Many factories are located along the Caspian coast and in Esfahan. Iran's handwoven carpets are prized throughout the world. Making these rugs is an important source of income in **rural** areas of the country.

700,000
Number of automobile factory workers in Iran.

3.6 Million
Number of barrels of oil that can be produced daily in Iran. (572 million L)

39% Portion of Iran's **gross domestic product** generated by industry.

Refineries in Iran process the country's oil into products such as gasoline and diesel fuel.

GOODS AND SERVICES

Many Iranians have jobs in service industries. These are industries in which workers provide services to other people rather than produce goods. Service workers in Iran include tour guides, truck drivers, store clerks, government employees, teachers, doctors, lawyers, and restaurant chefs and waiters.

Both today and in the past, Iran's location has helped to make trade with other regions an important part of the economy. For centuries, Iran was part of an overland trade route called the Silk Road. Merchants traveling long distances between Europe and East Asia traded goods along the way. Today, the Persian Gulf is busy with ships carrying Iranian exports and bringing **imports** to the country.

Petroleum products make up 80 percent of the goods exported by Iran. China is the largest buyer of Iranian exports, followed by India, Turkey, and Japan. Iran's imports include materials for its manufacturing industries, such as machines, parts, and chemicals. The countries from which Iran buys the most imports are the United Arab Emirates, China, Turkey, and South Korea.

49% Portion of Iranian workers who have service jobs.

$71 Billion Amount of Iran's imports in 2015.

40% Portion of imports received from the United Arab Emirates.

$79 Billion Total value of goods exported by Iran in 2015.

About 90 percent of Iran's oil exports are shipped from the port at Khark Island in the Persian Gulf.

INDIGENOUS PEOPLES

People have been living in Iran for about 100,000 years. Early peoples lived in caves and rock shelters. They survived by hunting animals and gathering plant foods. These people made weapons and tools from stone and animal bones. They created petroglyphs, or images drawn or carved in rock.

In 1951, an **archaeologist** found a cave in southwestern Iran's Zagros Mountains that had been used by ancient peoples. When Kunji Cave was excavated, archaeologists discovered evidence of prehistoric campfires. They also found pottery and tools in the cave.

Another important site was discovered on the island of Qeshm, in the Strait of Hormuz. In 2005, archaeologists found handmade stone tools. They believe that **nomadic** hunters made the tools at least 40,000 years ago.

In 2009, a large mound was discovered in the Zagros Mountains. Inside the mound, archaeologists found stone tools such as grinders and mortars. These were used to process grain about 11,000 years ago. The mound is one of the oldest agricultural sites discovered anywhere in the world.

1963
Year that excavation began at Kunji Cave.

6,000 BC Time when farming villages had been established throughout the Iranian plateau.

1937 Year the country's main archaeological museum, now part of the National Museum of Iran, opened in Tehran.

Rock art created between 17,000 and 4,500 years ago has been found in the Zagros Mountains.

EARLY SETTLERS

A bout 3,000 years ago, two groups called the Persians and the Medes settled in what is now Iran. They began to farm there. This led to more settlement, and powerful empires began to grow.

In the sixth century BC, a Persian king, Cyrus the Great, defeated the Median Empire. He united Median and Persian lands and became ruler of a new Achaemenian Empire. It would grow to become one of the largest empires in world history. At its height, the Achaemenian Empire stretched from Iran to Turkey and Egypt in the west. It reached as far east as India.

The Achaemenian Empire lasted for more than 200 years. Emperors who followed Cyrus included Darius I and Xerxes I. In 330 BC, Alexander the Great of Greece conquered the Achaemenian Empire. The Greeks ruled Persia for almost a century. Then, the Parthians, who lived in what is now northeastern Iran, created a new Persian Empire. This lasted for several hundred years. The Parthians were conquered by another group of Persians called the Sasanians. Sasanian rule continued from AD 224 to 651.

518 BC
Year that Darius I began to build the city of Persepolis.

49 Million Estimated population of the Achaemenian Empire in 480 BC.

1,500 Miles
Length of the Achaemenian Royal Road, leading from the western end of the empire to the capital at Persepolis. (2,400 km)

One of Cyrus the Great's most important conquests occurred in 539 BC, when his army captured the city of Babylon, in what is now Iraq.

THE AGE OF EXPLORATION

In the 7th century AD, a powerful new force, Islam, emerged in the Middle East. Islam began in what is now Saudi Arabia. Then, Muslim nomads began to conquer other parts of the Middle East region. They reached Persia in 637 and defeated the Sasanians in a series of battles over the next several years. The Muslim conquerors brought their religion to Persia.

Kubatcha pottery, first made centuries ago, is an example of how Islamic designs were used to decorate household items.

Over the next 600 years, a series of rulers battled for control. At different times, parts of Persia fell under Arab or Turkish rule. The many cultures coming together in the region continued to form a uniquely Persian culture.

In the 13th century, a new group arrived in Persia. From their homeland in eastern Asia, Mongol invaders swept across the continent. In the name of their emperor, Genghis Khan, the Mongols conquered Persia. Mongol culture mixed with the Persian, Arab, and Turkish cultures in the area.

The Mongols' fast and powerful horses helped them conquer Persia and many other lands.

In the 1500s, the Safavid **dynasty** united Persia. The Shiite form of Islam became the state religion. During the 1800s, European countries began to play a larger role in Persian affairs. Persia lost some of its territory to Russia. Trade with Great Britain led to the growth of British influence. Persia began to buy industrial goods from European countries.

In the early 20th century, countries such as Russia and Great Britain used their loans of money to Persia's government to influence the country's shahs, or rulers. A **nationalist** movement began to grow in Persia. The people wanted more control over their own country and government. In 1906, Persian leaders created a **constitution**. The constitution gave some of the shah's powers to an elected parliament, or legislature.

The parliament's power did not last for long. During World War I, which was fought from 1914 to 1918, Persia was the site of heavy fighting. Persian forces fought on the side of British and Russian troops against Turkish forces. In 1921, a Persian military leader named Reza Khan took control of the government in a **coup d'état**. He had himself crowned shah in 1925 and became known as Reza Shah Pahlavi.

1219–1223
Period of attacks on Persia by Genghis Khan's Mongol army.

16
Number of years Reza Khan was shah.

1935 Year that Persia changed its name to Iran.

The fortress of Bam, in southeastern Persia, was built during the Safavid dynasty and was an important trading center on the Silk Road.

POPULATION

I ran is home to more than 82 million people. It is the second-most-populated country in the Middle East, after Egypt. Iran's population is not evenly distributed. A fairly small number of Iranians make their homes in the country's deserts or mountains, where living conditions can be difficult. Almost three-fourths of Iranians live in urban areas, or cities and towns.

More than 10 percent of the country's population lives in Tehran. About 3 million people live in the city of Mashhad. Esfahan, Karaj, Shiraz, and Tabriz are each home to more than one million residents. Many Iranian cities are located at the foot of a mountain range. Often, underground mountain water sources provide a city's water supply. Some cities, such as Shiraz, are located at an oasis.

Many Iranians have access to good health care and schools. The average **life expectancy** in Iran is 71 years. This is about the same as the average for all people worldwide. Life expectancy in Iran has risen steadily since the 1960s. About 87 percent of Iranians over the age of 15 can read and write. This is about equal to the global average.

16 Number of countries in the world with larger populations than Iran's.

5% Percentage of Iranians who are age 65 or older.

24% Portion of Iran's population under the age of 15.

The Vakil Bazaar, or market, in Shiraz is often crowded with shoppers. Its high ceilings keep it cool in summer and warm in winter.

POLITICS AND GOVERNMENT

Reza Shah Pahlavi left office in 1941 and was followed by his son, Mohammad Reza Pahlavi. The two men brought many changes to the country, including making the educational and legal systems more similar to those in Europe and North America. They also increased women's rights.

However, their rule became unpopular with many Iranians. They governed as **dictators** and jailed people who opposed them. Countries such as Great Britain and the United States had a great deal of influence with the government. Many Iranians believed that changes in the country went against the values of Islam. In 1979, a revolution overthrew Mohammad Reza Pahlavi. Religious leader **Ayatollah** Ruhollah Khomeini took power. He declared Iran an Islamic republic, a type of government based on religious laws. Religious leaders approved a new constitution.

Under the constitution, Iran's most powerful official is the Supreme Leader, who is appointed by a group of religious leaders. Ayatollah Khomeini was the first Supreme Leader. Iran has an elected president and an elected legislature, called the Majles. Their powers are limited compared to the Supreme Leader.

4 Years
Length of the president's term in office.

1963 Year that women gained the right to vote in Iran.

444 Days
Length of time 52 Americans were held captive after anti-American protesters took over the U.S. embassy in Tehran on November 4, 1979, following the revolution that overthrew the shah.

Ayatollah Ali Khamenei became Iran's Supreme Leader in 1989, following the death of Ayatollah Khomeini.

CULTURAL GROUPS

Persian is the most common cultural background in Iran. Persian, or Farsi, is Iran's official language. A number of other cultural groups and languages are found across the country. A large group of Kurdish people lives in northwestern Iran, sometimes called Kurdistan. Most Kurds speak Kurdish. The Baloch people live in eastern Iran. Many of the members of this cultural group speak Balochi, which is similar to Persian. People of Turkish and Arab origins also live in Iran.

Road signs to Tehran are written in English as well as Persian, since the city is an international destination.

More than 99 percent of the country's people are Muslim. About 90 percent of these people follow Shiite Islam. The other 10 percent follow the religion's other main branch, Sunni Islam. These figures are the opposite of the percentages for Muslims worldwide, where about 90 percent are Sunni and 10 percent are Shiite. Iran is home to more Shiite Muslims than any other nation.

In many places in Iran, Shiite wedding practices remain as they have been for centuries. In Bandar-e Kong on the Persian Gulf, brides await their wedding in a room decorated for the occasion.

Some followers of various other religions can be found in Iran. There are small groups of Christians and Jews. Some people still follows the ancient Persian faith of Zoroastrianism.

The Islamic religious laws called sharia greatly influence life in Iran. Codes of conduct and morality discussed in the Quran, Islam's holy book, have been adopted into the country's legal system. These rules have an especially strong impact on women. Dress codes require women in Iran to cover their hair and the skin on their arms and legs when in public. For both men and women, drinking alcoholic beverages is not permitted.

Iranians celebrate several Islamic holidays. They also celebrate the Persian New Year, or Noruz. The new year holiday is spent visiting relatives and giving gifts.

Noruz began as the Zoroastrian New Year. Feasting is part of the celebration. It is customary to set the table with seven foods that have names beginning with the letter *s* in Persian.

Cultural Groups BY THE NUMBERS

Almost 7 Million
Estimated number of Kurdish people in Iran.

About 1 Million
Number of Iranians in the Baloch cultural group.

MARCH 20 OR 21
Date of the Persian New Year.

ARTS AND ENTERTAINMENT

Marjane Satrapi's *Persepolis* won the award known as the Jury Prize at the 2007 Cannes Film Festival in France.

The arts have a rich history in Iran. Weaving may be the best-known Iranian art form. Persian carpets are celebrated for their high quality and colorful patterns. Each region of the country creates carpets with unique designs.

Persian and Iranian writers have also been recognized for centuries. In the past, authors such as Ferdowsi and Rumi wrote **epic** poetry about the history of Persia. Modern writers include Sadeq Hedayat, Shahrnoush Parsipour, and Marjane Satrapi. Hedayat is credited with introducing **modernist** writing to Iran. He combined this style with Persian folklore. In Parsipour's novel *Women Without Men*, she writes about issues women face in Iranian society.

Satrapi writes graphic novels. Her series *Persepolis* is about growing up in Tehran at the time of the 1979 revolution. In 2007, Satrapi turned *Persepolis* into a film. Both Parsipour and Satrapi no longer live in Iran. The Iranian government does not always allow authors to write what they wish.

In Kurdistan, Seneh carpets are made in the city of Sanandaj. Some carpets have hexagonal, or six-sided, designs within a diamond shape.

Iranian architecture has influenced building styles around the world. Stone buildings and sculptures at **UNESCO** World Heritage Sites such as Persepolis reflect Persia's power in the ancient world. Beginning in the 7ᵗʰ century, some of the world's great palaces and mosques were constructed. These can be found in cities such as Esfahan and Shiraz. In 1967, the National Council for Iranian Architecture was created. It encourages Iranian architects to use traditional styles in their designs. The Azadi Tower is one example of a recent structure in a traditional style.

Tehran's many museums include the Golestan Palace Museum. It exhibits Iranian art and **antiquities**. Ancient and modern treasures can also be found in the National Museum of Iran and the Negarestan Garden and Museum. The Negarestan displays some artworks outdoors in its large garden. In 1977, the Tehran Museum of Modern Art opened.

Iran has a large film industry. Iranian movies are shown at international film festivals around the world. In 2012, *A Separation*, about a couple in Tehran seeking a divorce, won the Academy Award for best foreign-language film.

Works by present-day Iranian painters are displayed, and can be bought, at art galleries in Tehran and other cities.

Arts and Entertainment BY THE NUMBERS

990 Number of chapters in Ferdowsi's epic poem "Shahnameh" (Book of Kings).

$34 MILLION Price paid at an auction in 2013 for a Persian carpet, the highest known amount ever spent for a rug.

1984 Year the Golestan Palace Museum opened.

SPORTS

Many types of sports are popular in Iran, and Iranian athletes have had success at international tournaments. However, after the 1979 revolution, the government made it more difficult for Iranian athletes to compete. Government funding for training facilities was reduced. For a time, women were not allowed to take part in many events. Since the 1990s, more women are participating in professional sports and international competitions, although they must follow Islamic dress code requirements. Women's access to sports stadiums in Iran is limited.

Iranian Niloufar Mardani competed in the women's 10,000-meter roller sports race during the 2010 Asian Games, held in Guangzhou, China.

Soccer is many Iranians' favorite sport. In 1978, Iran's national men's team qualified for the first time for the World Cup tournament, in which the world's best national teams compete. Iran did not reach the World Cup tournament again until 1998. In that year, Iran won a World Cup game for the first time, with 2–1 upset victory over a favored United States team. Iran also qualified for the men's World Cup in 2006 and 2014.

Iran's national men's soccer team often wears red uniforms when competing in international events.

At international events, Iranian athletes have won a number of medals in wrestling and weightlifting. The roots of this success go back thousands of years. Zurkhaneh has been a popular sport in Iran since ancient times. The name means "house of strength." A martial art first practiced long ago is called Varzesh-e-Bastani. It combines wrestling, bodybuilding, and meditation. These activities are still practiced and highly respected. Taking part in them has helped Iranian athletes to develop their skills.

At the 2016 Summer Olympics in Rio de Janeiro, Brazil, Iranian athletes won three gold medals. Kianoush Rostami and Sohrab Moradi won gold in weightlifting. Rostami broke his own world record and set a new Olympic record. Hassan Aliazam Yazdanicharati won a gold medal in wrestling. Iranian wrestlers also brought home one silver and three bronze medals. Kimia Alizadeh Zenoorin was Iran's only woman to win a medal. She took the bronze in taekwondo.

Zurkhaneh combines weightlifting with other activities such as wrestling and dance.

396 KILOGRAMS
Weightlifting world record set by Kianoush Rostami in 2016.

64 Number of Iranian athletes who competed at the 2016 Olympics.

1948 Year that Iran first competed in the Olympic Games.

Mapping Iran

We use many tools to interpret maps and to understand the locations of features such as cities, states, lakes, and rivers. The map below has many tools to help interpret information on the map of Iran.

Map of Iran

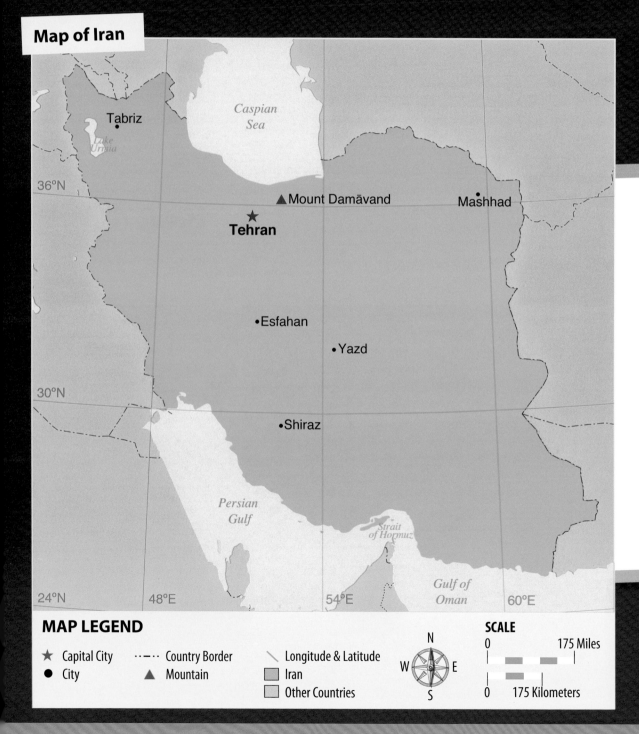

MAP LEGEND

★ Capital City
● City

----- Country Border
▲ Mountain

╲ Longitude & Latitude
▨ Iran
▨ Other Countries

N
W   E
S

SCALE
0 _____ 175 Miles

0 _____ 175 Kilometers

Mapping Tools

- The compass rose shows north, south, east, and west. The points in between represent northeast, northwest, southeast, and southwest.
- The map scale shows that the distances on a map represent much longer distances in real life. If you measure the distance between objects on a map, you can use the map scale to calculate the actual distance in miles or kilometers between those two points.

- The lines of latitude and longitude are long lines that appear on maps. The lines of latitude run east to west and measure how far north or south of the equator a place is located. The lines of longitude run north to south and measure how far east or west of the Prime Meridian a place is located. A location on a map can be found by using the two numbers where latitude and longitude meet. This number is called a coordinate and is written using degrees and direction. For example, the city of Tehran would be found at 35°N and 51°E on a map.

Map It!

Using the map and the appropriate tools, complete the activities below.

Locating with latitude and longitude
1. Which body of water is located at 38°N and 45°E?
2. Which mountain is located at 36°N and 52°E?
3. Which city is found at 32°N and 51°E?

Distances between points
4. Using the map scale and a ruler, calculate the approximate distance between Tehran and Shiraz.
5. Using the map scale and a ruler, calculate the approximate distance between Mashhad and Yazd.
6. Using the map scale and a ruler, calculate the distance between Tabriz and Esfahan.

Quiz Time

Test your knowledge of Iran by answering these questions.

1 What is the name of Iran's largest desert?

2 What portion of Iran's border is seacoast?

3 What was the main religion in Persia before Islam?

4 Which Middle Eastern country has more oil reserves than Iran?

5 What city was the capital of the Achaemenian Empire?

6 What are the two most valuable natural resources in Iran?

7 In what year was Kunji Cave first excavated?

8 What empire did Cyrus the Great defeat to form the Achaemenian Empire?

9 In what year did Ayatollah Khomeini take power?

10 Which branch of Islam is followed by most people in Iran?

ANSWERS
1. Kavir Desert
2. One-third
3. Zoroastrianism
4. Saudi Arabia
5. Persepolis
6. Oil and natural gas
7. 1963
8. Median Empire
9. 1979
10. Shiite Islam

Key Words

adapted: changed to make it easier to live in a place or situation
antiquities: objects created in ancient times
archaeologist: a scientist who studies past human life and activities
architecture: the styles used for designing buildings
ayatollah: a high-ranking Shiite Muslim leader
constitution: a written document stating a country's or area's basic principles and laws
coup d'état: a sudden overthrow of a government, bringing a new group into power
dictators: rulers who have absolute power and allow people very little freedom
dynasty: a series of rulers from the same family and the area they govern
economy: the wealth and resources of a country or area
elevation: the height of land above sea level
empires: large territories headed by a single ruler

endangered: at risk of becoming extinct, or dying out completely
epic: related to a long poem that describes historic events and heroic actions
exports: goods sold to another country or area
gross domestic product: the total value of the goods and services a country or area produces in a year
imports: goods that are bought from another country
Islamic: having to do with Islam, the religion of Muslims
life expectancy: the number of years that a person can expect to live
modernist: a style of writing developed in the 20th century, focused on reactions to the changing world
nationalist: relating to a person or group working for national independence or strong national government
nomadic: moving from place to place rather than living in a permanent home

oases: areas in a desert that have a source of water
plateau: an area of usually flat land that is higher than the surrounding land
reserves: the amount of a mineral available for future use
rural: relating to the countryside
sanctions: restrictions on trade and other economic activity that countries impose on a nation to try to convince that nation to change certain policies
Shiite: referring to one of the two main branches of Islam and the branch followed by most Muslims in Iran
species: groups of individuals with common characteristics
tectonic plates: large sections of Earth's surface that are slowly moving
UNESCO: the United Nations Educational, Scientific, and Cultural Organization, whose main goals are to promote world peace and eliminate poverty through education, science, and culture

Index

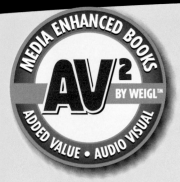

Log on to www.av2books.com

AV² by Weigl brings you media enhanced books that support active learning. Go to www.av2books.com, and enter the special code found on page 2 of this book. You will gain access to enriched and enhanced content that supplements and complements this book. Content includes video, audio, weblinks, quizzes, a slide show, and activities.

AV² Online Navigation

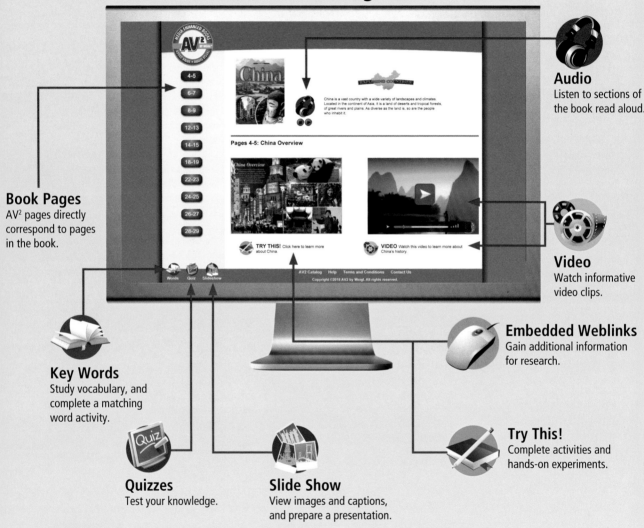

Audio
Listen to sections of the book read aloud.

Book Pages
AV² pages directly correspond to pages in the book.

Video
Watch informative video clips.

Key Words
Study vocabulary, and complete a matching word activity.

Embedded Weblinks
Gain additional information for research.

Try This!
Complete activities and hands-on experiments.

Quizzes
Test your knowledge.

Slide Show
View images and captions, and prepare a presentation.

AV² was built to bridge the gap between print and digital. We encourage you to tell us what you like and what you want to see in the future.

Sign up to be an AV² Ambassador at www.av2books.com/ambassador.